Dear little Linds,

Your momma and I had great fun traveling around. Bethany College and getting into fun — ask her about pretzels the size of your head! Maybe she'll even let you call her Moose! I love you, little one, + your momma! I love you dear! BethAnn Shaffer

Dear Mac Baby,

The love, support + prayers we all have for you is immense + ever-growing with each day! I cannot wait to meet + spoil you — just as your own momma showers her loved ones with so much care + affection. I wish you all the best + know that you have a piece of my heart — you, little girl, are never alone.

Tons of love, Bethany Lewis

(P.S. - Here's a few books about the fun times you can have in TX :)

Goodnight Dallas

Enjoy Dallas ⭐

Jennifer Drez

Written by
Jennifer Drez

Illustrated by
Lisa Voight

Goodnight Dallas
Library of Congress Control Number: 2014914634
ISBN-13: 978-0-9886023-1-1
First Edition- 2014
Illustrations by Lisa Carrington Voight using acrylic paint on canvas.
Graphic Design by Cynthia Wahl
Printed in Canada

To order additional copies of this book, please visit www.goodnightdallas.com

Goodnight Dallas is dedicated to my wonderful
husband David, our three sons, David, Phillip and Patrick
and to the people of Dallas. It is my hope that through the
text and illustrations, children and adults alike will learn
more about Dallas and all it has to offer, be inspired
to visit the places in the book and share their
experiences with others.

The sun is setting on the Dallas skyline.

Let's say goodnight as the stars begin to shine.

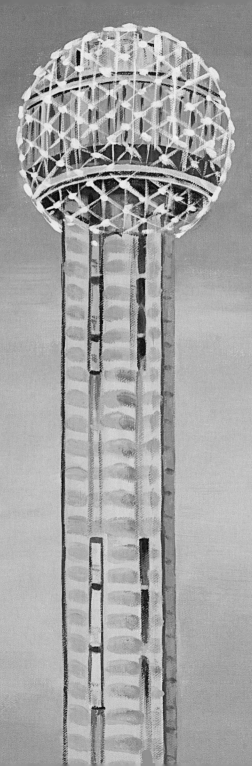

Goodnight Reunion Tower
and to the Adolphus.

Goodnight to the Magnolia Hotel with its flying red Pegasus.

Goodnight to Old Red, Dealey Plaza and the Sixth Floor Museum.

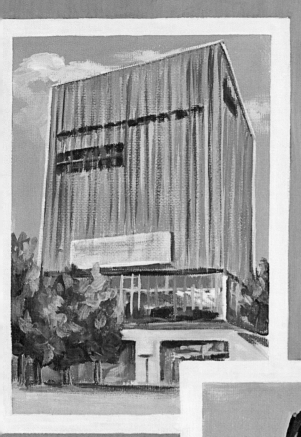

Goodnight to the Winspear,
the Wyly and the Meyerson.

Goodnight to the DMA, the Crow Collection
and the Nasher's amazing sculpture.

**Goodnight to dinosaurs,
musical stairs and
inspiring architecture.**

Goodnight to Klyde Warren Park where we exercise, eat and play.

Goodnight to the
Aquarium,
a great sloth,
sea creatures
and stingrays.

Goodnight to fun times at the Majestic Theatre and the Latino Cultural Center.

Goodnight to the Farmer's Market, fruits, veggies and flowering planters.

Goodnight to the Bishop Arts District,

the Trinity River and the Margaret Hunt Hill Bridge that stands so tall.

Goodnight to
the mayor,
City Hall, police
and firefighters.

Thank you for
leading and
protecting us all.

**Goodnight to the McKinney Avenue Trolley
and to Katy Trail where we walk, skip and run.**

Goodnight to ducks swimming
in Turtle Creek,
beautiful azaleas and
a splashing fountain.

Goodnight SMU, The Meadows Museum and the Bush Library.

Goodnight to Kuby's,
Highland Park Village
and coke floats at
the Pharmacy.

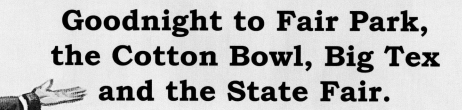

**Goodnight to Fair Park,
the Cotton Bowl, Big Tex
and the State Fair.**

Goodnight Pioneer Plaza,
the cowboys and
cattle we see there.

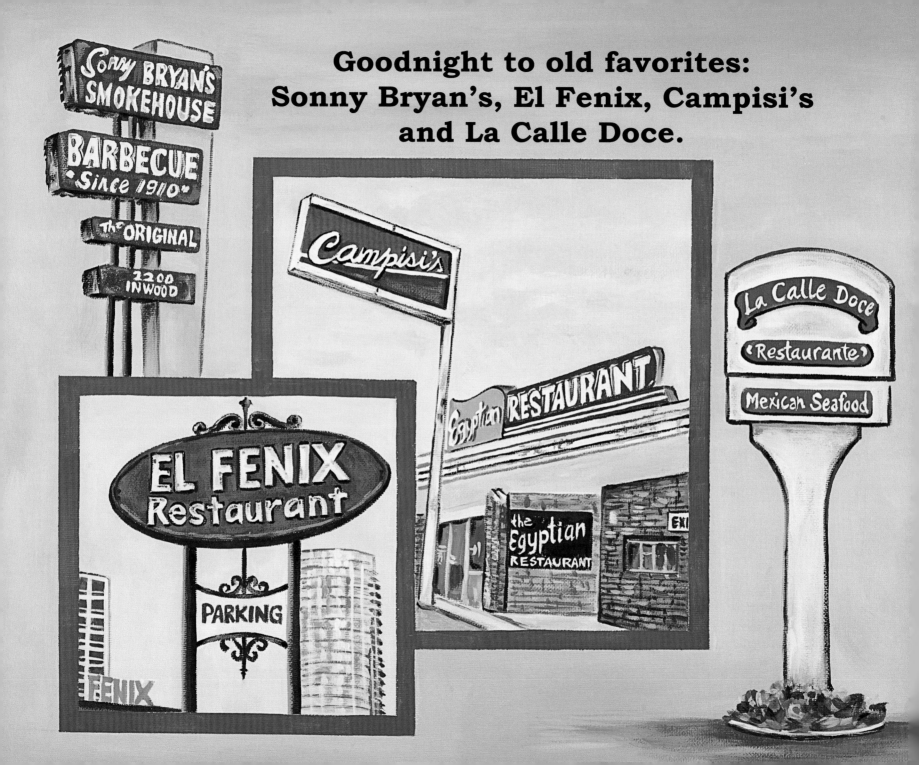

Goodnight to old favorites:
Sonny Bryan's, El Fenix, Campisi's
and La Calle Doce.

Goodnight Love Field
with planes taking off to fly far away.

DALLAS LOVE FIELD

Goodnight White Rock Lake, marathon runners, cyclists and rowers.

Goodnight to the Arboretum,
the Children's Adventure Garden
and colorful flowers.

Goodnight
to tigers,
penguins and
giraffes at the
Dallas Zoo.

Goodnight to golfers at the Byron Nelson Championship, too.

Goodnight to Neiman Marcus, the NorthPark slides and shops selling everything from cupcakes to toys.

Goodnight to victory celebrations for the Mavericks, FC Dallas, Stars, Rangers and Cowboys!

The sun has set, the stars shine bright.

Sweet dreams, Dallas. Goodnight!

ACKNOWLEDGEMENTS

Dallas is a diverse, culturally rich city with a dynamic history. My goal is that this book will help visitors and residents celebrate everything that Dallas has to offer. I am grateful to the many people that helped bring this book to life. Everyone involved, including people in local government, non-profit leadership and local residents, have a great love for Dallas and pride in its history. Dallas is an amazing city to raise a family, live, visit, play and work. I hope the people of Dallas are proud of *Goodnight Dallas* and share it with others.

---- ★ ----

DALLAS

Dallas was founded in 1841 when John Neely Bryan laid claim to 640 acres and sketched out a town plan. In 1846, Dallas County was formed and the city of Dallas was incorporated on February 2, 1856. Located on the Trinity River, Dallas quickly became the center of trade in cotton, grain and buffalo. At one point, Dallas was the world's leading inland cotton market.

The area continued to grow and attract more attention over the years. Railroads arrived in the 1870s, Neiman Marcus in 1907, the Federal Reserve Bank in 1914, SMU in 1915, Dallas Love Field Airport in 1917 and the Texas Centennial Exposition in 1936.

Over the years, Dallas became a financial center for the oil industry and is also well-known for its role in banking, transportation and computer technology. Today, Dallas is a leading corporate destination embraced for its entrepreneurial spirit, style, innovation and opportunity. Its sport teams, cultural institutions, parks and great shopping all make Dallas a favorite tourist destination.

Reunion Tower

This 50-story observation tower in downtown Dallas was designed by Welton Becker & Associates and was completed in 1978. It is adjacent to the Hyatt Regency Hotel and is one of the most recognizable landmarks in Dallas. Reunion Tower is known for its 360 degree observation deck with interactive activities and a revolving restaurant and bar.

Adolphus Hotel

Located in downtown Dallas, the Adolphus Hotel is an upscale hotel and Dallas landmark. It opened in October 1912 and is the oldest hotel in Dallas. It was built by Adolphus Busch, founder of the Anheuser–Busch Company. Designed by Thomas Barnett in a Beaux Arts style, the Adolphus has a long list of famous and notable hotel guests that includes musicians, business leaders, presidents and world leaders.

Magnolia Hotel and the Pegasus

This building originally was headquarters to the Magnolia Petroleum Company. It is best known for its trademark Pegasus that was erected on the roof in 1934 in celebration of the American Petroleum Institute's annual meeting. The Pegasus remains a well-known landmark and endearing Dallas icon.

Old Red Museum of Dallas County History & Culture

The building that houses the Old Red Museum was built in 1892 as the Dallas County Courthouse. Designed by Max Orlapp, Jr. in the Richardson Romanesque style of architecture, it was built with red sandstone with marble accents. In 1966, a newer courthouse replaced Old Red and the building now serves as a local history museum.

Dealey Plaza

Dealey Plaza, completed in 1940 as a WPA project, is located on land donated to the City of Dallas by Sarah Horton Cockrell. It is named for George Dealey, a civic leader and early publisher of the Dallas Morning News. Dealey Plaza is best known as the location of the assassination of John F. Kennedy on November 22, 1963.

The Sixth Floor Museum at Dealey Plaza

The Sixth Floor Museum is located on the sixth and seventh floors of the former Texas School Book Depository. The Museum chronicles the life, death and legacy of President John F. Kennedy. It aims to be an impartial, multi-generational forum for exploring the events surrounding the assassination of President Kennedy.

Margot and Bill Winspear Opera House

The Winspear Opera House, home to the Dallas Opera and the Texas Ballet Theater, is located in the Arts District. The Winspear also partners with local and national organizations to present a variety of cultural programming. The building was designed by Foster and Partners as a 21st century interpretation of a traditional opera house.

Dee and Charles Wyly Theatre

The Wyly Theatre and its impressive architecture was designed by Joshua Prince-Ramos and Rem Koolhaas. The theatre can seat up to 600 people and can transform into many different configurations, allowing for incredible performance flexibility. The Wyly serves as the venue for the Dallas Theater Center, Dallas Black Dance Theatre and the Anita Martinez Ballet Folklorico.

Morton H. Meyerson Symphony Center

The Meyerson, which was designed by distinguished architect I.M. Pei, opened in 1989. It is home to the Dallas Symphony Orchestra, the Turtle Creek Chorale, the Dallas Wind Symphony and the Greater Dallas Youth Orchestra. The Meyerson is well-known for its impressive design and unsurpassed acoustics.

Dallas Museum of Art

The Dallas Museum of Art (DMA) is located in a building designed by Edward Larrabee Barnes in the Dallas Arts District. The DMA's collection began in 1903 as the Dallas Art Association and now consists of more than 24,000 important objects, dating from the third millennium B.C. to the present. The Museum is well-known for its role in the community, free admission and its Center for Creative Connections.

Crow Collection of Asian Art

Trammell and Margaret Crow opened the Crow Collection of Asian Art in 1998 as a permanent museum. The Museum showcases the art and cultures of China, Japan, India and Southeast Asia. It is considered one of the finest museums in the United States focused on Asian Art.

Nasher Sculpture Center

The Nasher Sculpture Center opened in 2003 and is home to one of the finest collections of modern and contemporary sculptures in the world. Designed by architect Renzo Piano in collaboration with landscape architect Peter Walker, the museum aims to be a focal point and catalyst for the study, installation, conservation and appreciation of sculpture. The collection consists of more than 300 sculptures dating from the late 19th century to the present.

Perot Museum of Nature and Science

The Perot Museum of Nature and Science offers dynamic experiences to stimulate curiosity in visitors of all ages. The extraordinary building, exhibit halls and outdoor spaces all serve as living science lessons through hands-on discovery. The building and landscape design demonstrate scientific principles and serve as examples of sustainability and conservation.

Klyde Warren Park

Klyde Warren Park serves as a central gathering space for Dallas and its visitors. It is a five-acre urban deck park built over Woodall Rogers Freeway. The park includes a performance pavilion, walking trails, food trucks, children's park, dog park and a games area.

The Dallas World Aquarium

Located near the Historic West End, the Dallas World Aquarium, opened in 1992. The upper level is a reproduction of the Orinoco Rainforest, which has one of the only public displays of three-toed sloths. The lower level features aquariums with fish and sea animals from around the world and includes the Mundo Maya exhibit filled with plants and animals important to the ancient Mayan culture.

Majestic Theatre

The Majestic Theatre opened in 1921 and is one of the most elegant and historic performing arts spaces in the Southwestern United States. The Majestic hosts shows ranging from nationally touring concerts and comedy acts to locally-produced cultural events and fundraisers.

Latin Cultural Center

The Latin Cultural Center is a multidisciplinary arts center designed by architect Ricardo Legorreta. It serves as a regional catalyst for the preservation, development and promotion of Latino and Hispanic arts and culture.

Dallas Farmer's Market

The Dallas Farmer's Market opened in the late 1800s and continues to be a large public market in the center of the city. The market offers a wide variety of fruits and vegetables from local farmers, wholesale dealers and produce dealers. There are seasonal festivals, cooking classes, yard sales and an adjacent floral and garden market.

Bishop Arts District

The Bishop Arts District is a small shopping and entertainment district located in North Oak Cliff. The area is known for street festivals and a large selection of restaurants, independent boutique shops and galleries.

Margaret Hunt Hill Bridge

The Margaret Hunt Hill Bridge is a defining landmark of the Trinity River Corridor designed by renowned architect and engineer Santiago Calatrava. The bridge connects Woodall Rogers Freeway to Singleton Boulevard in West Dallas. It was built to spur economic development and foster unity within Dallas by connecting the North and South Oak Cliff neighborhoods.

Dallas City Hall and Park Plaza

Dallas City Hall and Park Plaza were designed by world-renowned architect I.M. Pei. The building is an inverted pyramid design with a reflecting pool and notable sculptures adorning the area. It serves as the seat of the city's municipal government.

La Calle Doce

In September 1981, Oscar and Laura Sanchez welcomed the first customers into La Calle Doce in Oak Cliff. As a twenty-year veteran of numerous restaurant kitchens, Oscar had developed a vision for a restaurant of his own featuring seafood and Tex-Mex made with the freshest ingredients. Since then, La Calle Doce has been serving visitors from Dallas and beyond.

McKinney Avenue Trolley

The McKinney trolley is run by the McKinney Avenue Transit Authority. It recreates the trolley system that served Dallas from the early to mid-20th century. Restored vintage trolleys provide a great way to see and explore Uptown Dallas. The car in the illustration is Car 122, Crescent Rose or "Rosie," which was built in 1909 and is the oldest streetcar in daily service in the United States.

Katy Trail

Katy Trail is a jogging, walking and cycling path that follows the path of the old Missouri-Kansas-Texas Railroad, known as the MKT or the Katy. The trail runs through the Uptown and Oaklawn areas and provides a way of connecting various city parks. It is funded by the Friends of Katy Trail, a non-profit organization founded in 1997.

Turtle Creek

Turtle Creek is a scenic tributary of the Trinity River starting in Reverchon Park and winding through Oak Lawn and into Highland Park. The creek is surrounded by beautiful neighborhoods, fountains and landscaped areas perfect for a stroll or picnic. The area is maintained by the Turtle Creek Association.

Southern Methodist University

Founded in 1911 by the Methodist Church, Southern Methodist University (SMU) is a highly-regarded private academic institution. The campus is home to the George W. Bush Presidential Library and Museum and the Meadows Museum. SMU's sports teams play in the Division 1 American Athletic Conference. The team mascot is a Mustang pony, named Peruna.

Meadows Museum

The Meadows Museum is located on the SMU campus and has one of the largest and most comprehensive collections of Spanish Art outside of Spain. The collection was amassed by Algur H.Meadows, who gave the funds to SMU to construct and endow a museum to house his vast collection as a unique resource for local schools, colleges and the community.

George W. Bush Presidential Library and Museum

The Bush Presidential Library and Museum on the SMU campus houses the records of the life and career of George W. Bush, the 43rd President of the United States. The collection encourages a better understanding of the Presidency and American history and provides a multi-generational, interactive and educational experience for the entire family.

Kuby's Sausage House

In 1961, Karl Kuby immigrated to Dallas from Germany and opened Kuby's Sausage House, Inc. in Snider Plaza near SMU. His goal was to introduce Texas to the tradition and the taste of fine specialty sausages and foods of his childhood. Kuby's recipes use only the finest ingredients and have been handed down from father to son for more than 14 generations.

Highland Park Village

This upscale shopping center is a National Historical Landmark. It opened in 1931 as the first self-contained shopping center in America. Its classic architecture, fine shopping and restaurants make it a great destination for residents and tourists alike.

Highland Park Soda Fountain
Highland Park Soda Fountain, originally Highland Park Pharmacy, opened in 1912. Locals still refer to the establishment as the Pharmacy and the best place to go for a great grilled cheese or an old-fashioned milkshake. Historical newspaper clippings dating back to its opening adorn the walls, providing informative and entertaining reading material.

Fair Park
Fair Park is a National Historic Landmark located on 277 acres and is the largest collection of Art Deco exposition style architecture in the United States. It is home to seven museums and six performing arts facilities, including Music Hall, Texas Discovery Gardens, Gexa Energy Pavilion, the African-American Museum and the Cotton Bowl Stadium. Fair Park has been home to the Texas State Fair since 1886.

State Fair of Texas
The State Fair, which started in 1886, is held in Fair Park and lasts for 24 days every year. It boasts a car show, carnival rides, football games at the Cotton Bowl, corny dogs, fried goodies and much more. The iconic Big Tex, a 55-foot tall cowboy, towers over the State Fair to greet and entertain visitors. The Fair also features the Texas Star, a 212-foot-tall ferris wheel.

Pioneer Plaza
Pioneer Plaza is a public park located in downtown Dallas featuring native plants and trees along with a large bronze longhorn cattle drive sculpture by Robert Summers. The sculpture commemorates the trails that brought early settlers to Dallas and cattle to the market place.

Sonny Bryan's
In 1910, Elias Bryan opened Bryan's Barbeque. The family tradition continued in 1958 when his grandson opened Sonny Bryan's, which is well-known for its mouthwatering barbeque. Locals and tourists alike remember the school desks that are used as dining tables in some of their seven locations.

El Fenix
In 1918, Mexican immigrant Michael Martinez and his wife Faustina decided to turn their modest café in Dallas into El Fenix. The restaurant is renowned as the originator of "Tex-Mex Cuisine." Generations of families have grown up dining at the historic Dallas restaurant and continue to do so today.

Campisi's
Originally founded as Campisi's Egyptian Lounge by Joseph Campisi in 1946, the Campisi family continues to own and operate Campisi's more than six locations in Dallas and beyond. It is said that Campisi's is where Texas' first pizza was made and served.

Dallas Love Field
Love Field is a city-owned public airport. It was named by the United States Army in honor of Lt. Moss L. Love. The airport officially opened in 1917 as a flight training base for the U.S. Army Corps. Today, Love Field is a thriving airport that is also corporate headquarters to Southwest Airlines.

White Rock Lake
Built in response to a water shortage in Dallas in 1910, White Rock Lake now serves as a recreational lake for the city. It is surrounded by trails for hiking, running and bicycling as well as the Bath House Cultural Center and the Dallas Arboretum and Botanical Garden. The lake is a popular destination for rowing, sailing and fishing.

Dallas Arboretum and Botanical Garden
The Dallas Arboretum and Botanical Garden is one of the top ten display gardens in North America. With 66 acres on the shores of White Rock Lake, this nationally recognized garden has changeable displays four times a year, providing breathtaking color for visitors from March through November. The Rory Meyers Children's Adventure Garden, an eight-acre interactive garden, is the only children's educational garden of its scope in the world.

Dallas Zoo

Offering 106 acres of wildlife adventure, the Dallas Zoo is the largest zoological experience in Texas. Home to more than 2,000 animals representing over 400 species, the Zoo provides unique interactive activities such as giraffe and bird feedings, a mini Safari Express train, and a Monorail Safari tour. The zoo also features an eleven-acre Giants of the Savanna exhibit, the only place in North America where elephants share their habitat with giraffes, zebras and other African species.

Byron Nelson Championship

The Byron Nelson Championship is a PGA Tour golf tournament held each spring. Named after Byron Nelson, the tournament's first winner in 1944, it is organized and run by the Salesmanship Club of Dallas.

Neiman Marcus

The Neiman Marcus Company was established in 1907 in Dallas as a local specialty store. The company was founded by Herbert Marcus along with his sister Carrie M. Neiman and her husband Al Neiman. Neiman Marcus Group LTD LLC operations include the Specialty Retail Stores segment and the Online segment. The Specialty Retail Stores segment consists primarily of Neiman Marcus, Bergdorf Goodman and Last Call stores. The Online segment conducts direct to consumer operations under the Neiman Marcus, Horchow, CUSP, Last Call and Bergdorf Goodman brand names.

NorthPark Center

NorthPark Center was opened in 1965 and continues to be one of the premier shopping centers in America. The Center is a top tourist and shopping destination and features unique art as well as fun family activities such as the NorthPark slides, large sloped planters that children love to play on. Generations of children in Dallas have memories of running up the planters and sliding down while taking a break from shopping.

Dallas Mavericks

The Dallas Mavericks are members of the Southwest Division of the National Basketball Association (NBA). Since their inaugural season in 1980-81, the Mavericks have won three division titles, two conference championships and the NBA championship in 2011.

Dallas Stars

The Dallas Stars are a professional hockey team in the Central Division of the Western Conference of the National Hockey League (NHL). The Stars have won seven division titles, two President's trophies, two Western Conference Championships and a Stanley Cup Trophy in 1999.

FC Dallas

A member of Major League Soccer since its inception in 1996, FC Dallas is owned and operated by Hunt Sports Group. FC Dallas formerly known as the Dallas Burn soccer club, claimed the U.S. Open Cup in 1997 and earned its first Western Conference Championship in 2010. Renowned for its youth development system, FC Dallas is known for the "home grown" Dallas talent on its professional roster.

Texas Rangers

Originally franchised in 1961, the Arlington-based Texas Rangers are members of Major League Baseball's American League. Fans have enjoyed cheering them on to five AL West division titles and two AL championships.

Dallas Cowboys

The Dallas Cowboys are a professional football franchise playing in the East Division of the National Football Conference (NFC) of the National Football League (NFL). The Cowboys joined the NFL in 1960 as an expansion team. Five-time NFL champions, the Cowboys have had eight Super Bowl appearances and are the most valuable team in the NFL. They are the only team to record 20 straight winning seasons (1966-84).